STRETCHY
LESSON PLANS

October

Pat Miller

UpstartBooks

Fort Atkinson, Wisconsin

Dedicated to the school librarians of Tennessee,
particularly Nancy Dickinson, librarian at Hillsboro Elementary.

Credits:

Pages 23–25 adapted from *Stretchy Library Lessons: Seasons & Celebrations*, page 101.

Published by UpstartBooks
W5527 State Road 106
P.O. Box 800
Fort Atkinson, Wisconsin 53538-0800
1-800-448-4887

Contents

Works for Me!

 Useful Tips

Reminders

Humor

Appendix

Bibliography

Introduction

I was inspired to write this book by a woman at a library conference. After one of my presentations, we visited and she said, "I wish I could be a fly on the wall of your library—a fly with a notebook!" This series is for her, and for others who wonder what I do with my students "in the real world." It's also a good way for me to meet my annual resolution to get my lessons more organized!

If you're like me, you want to know how similar my situation is to yours. I'm a library media specialist in a suburban school of 940 students with a full-time aide. Our population is becoming more diverse, and we are adding more ELL classes from PreK through fifth grade. This is my nineteenth year as a librarian, preceded by 15 years as a classroom teacher. I've been a librarian at four schools in diverse situations.

I've been the only librarian for more than 1,200 elementary students (ten classes in most grades), and at a smaller school where many of my students' families were on welfare. I've been "in the rotation" when I taught classes to give the teachers their planning time. I've worked for avid library supporters and one who just wanted me to keep the kids quiet and the parents out of his office. I've worked without an aide, with an aide, and with a cadre of talented mother volunteers.

My current schedule is to see every child every week for check out, but to teach a fixed lesson to intermediates one week, and to their primary partners the next. In a typical month, that means only two lessons per grade. This is a Stretchy Lesson Plan book because I've included more lessons than one would use in a month. The lessons can stretch to fit a number of grade levels and will last for years without repeating if you have my kind of schedule. And best of all, the lessons are bound to trigger some great ideas of your own.

Do I Need These If I Have the Stretchy Library Lessons Books?

The SLL books are invaluable books of lessons for library skills, reading and reference activities, and multicultural and seasonal celebrations. One never has too many lessons from which to choose the best fit for his or her students. One difference is that this series is designed to give you not just lessons, but useful tips, forms, strategies, and reminders that I have developed or discovered over the years. This book is also an organizational tool, correlating additional ideas from the six books of the Stretchy Library Lessons series, the six Collaborative Bridges books, and the first 36 issues of *LibrarySparks*. Add these to your favorite lessons, adapting them to your own students.

Because the lessons from my other books are ones that I often use, those will be referenced in each book. You will have a list of six to eight additional lessons each month from my other books, as well as articles from the first four years of *LibrarySparks* magazine. I write these books not only for you, but also for myself, and I needed a resource that had all those things in one place for easy reference.

In this series, in one place, you have additional lessons for each month, along with useful tips, calendar correlations, forms, patterns, lots of books, and inspiration for your own planning. Whether you wonder how to find a lesson plan form that fits your schedule, how to run a successful book fair, or how to find good literature each week, the answers are here. This is not the definitive plan book, but it will guide you through the year, your library curriculum, and the special events that make your program more fun for students.

How to Use This Book

If you teach in the library, this book is for you. It will help you if you are a certified librarian with a master's degree and extensive experience or if you are a novice librarian in your first elementary library. I hope it will be especially helpful if you are an uncertified aide or generous volunteer. My hat is off to all of you who are constantly looking for ways to meet the needs of your students.

Lessons featured in this book represent many of the lessons I actually have used through the years. Sometimes teachable moments, special events, or collaborative units will bump lessons off your schedule, but these will give you a good start. Each book will include four lessons for grades K–2 and four for grades 3–5. I've also included a number of tips about how I do things in my library that seem to make life easier for my students and me, and might work for you as well.

Each lesson includes:

- **Objective(s):** Why teach this lesson? What student need will it address? How does it correlate to the curriculum?

- **Grades:** This indicates whether the lesson is intended for primary grades or intermediate grades. However, I'm confident that if you are using this book, you are also the person who can adapt any lesson and thrive in any situation.

- **Materials:** These are readily available or easily made and should be gathered before you teach the lesson.

- **Prepare in Advance:** If you teach all grades each day as I do, your lesson materials need to be well organized because there is little time between classes. This section tells you what needs to be made, purchased, or found before your class comes in.

- **Activity Directions:** My schedule is fixed at 45-minute classes, with a few bands of flexible time that can be scheduled by any teacher. The following lessons are designed for approximately 30 minutes and include all forms, worksheets, and patterns that you will need.

- **Resources:** This section lists books to use in place of the featured book or as companion books to it. Use them in a display, share them with teachers or plan extension lessons with them. Web sites are included here and can often be the basis for additional lessons. As I write, the books are in print and the Web sites are current. If you get an error message when using the address, perform a keyword search on the site title. If a book is out of print, check www.amazon.com

What's Happening This Month?

October is the month in which students are more settled in, autumn and cooler weather have arrived (at least in the northern states), and students begin to look forward to Halloween.

Set up a birthday display with "Thanks, __(author name)__, for the presents!" Display a fake birthday cake and attach birthday streamers, party hats, etc. If you don't have a handy bulletin board, use a science fair display board. Attach author pictures if you have them from Internet sites, publisher flyers, or book jackets. Then add the birthday books and encourage check out.

Look for 12 pages of birthday celebration ideas in *Stretchy Library Lessons: Seasons and Celebrations*. In your birthday display, you can feature the books by these authors:

Author Birthdays			
Karen Cushman	Oct. 4	Joseph Bruchac	Oct. 16
Robert Lawson	Oct. 4	Shel Silverstein	Oct. 18
Donald J. Sobol	Oct. 4	Dan Gutman	Oct. 19
David Shannon	Oct. 5	Ed Emberley	Oct. 19
Faith Ringgold	Oct. 8	John Erickson	Oct. 20
R. L. Stine	Oct. 8	Nikki Grimes	Oct. 20
Mike Thaler	Oct. 9	Gordon Korman	Oct. 23
Johanna Hurwitz	Oct. 9	Barbara Robinson	Oct. 24
James Marshall	Oct. 10	Steven Kellogg	Oct. 26
Daniel & Robert San Souci	Oct. 10	Valerie Worth	Oct. 29
Russell Freedman	Oct. 11	Eric Kimmell	Oct. 30
Miriam Cohen	Oct. 14	Katherine Paterson	Oct. 31

Meet these authors in the pages of *LibrarySparks* magazine:

Tony DiTerlizzi and Holly Black (3–5), October 2005

Denise Fleming (K–2), October 2003

James Howe (K–2, 3–5), October 2006

Jane Kurtz (3–5), October 2006 *

David Small (3–5), October 2004

*A Web Resource found on www.librarysparks.com.

October

- The second week of October is Fire Prevention Week. This commemorative week began after Mrs. O'Leary's cow kicked over a lighted lantern on October 8, 1871, which started the Great Chicago Fire and pointed up the need for improved fire prevention and fire protection.

- Daylight Savings Time ends at 2:00 a.m. of the last Sunday morning of the month. Time will "fall" back, resulting in an extra hour.

- October 27 is National Teddy Bear Day. Celebrate with the ideas in *LibrarySparks*, October 2005, pages 42–45. One of my favorite books to use on this day is *Famous Bears and Friends: One Hundred Years of Stories, Poems, Songs, and Heroics*. It explains how the teddy bear originated simultaneously on both sides of the Atlantic (and began the Ideal Toy Company in America). It also provides photos and pictures to accompany the true stories behind Winnie the Pooh, Paddington Bear, Corduroy, and other not so famous bears. In *Stretchy Library Lessons: Seasons and Celebrations*, there is a Jeopardy game with questions from *Famous Bears and Friends* on pages 47–49.

National Magic Day (Oct. 31)

- *Anansi and the Magic Stick* by Eric A. Kimmel. Holiday House, 2001.

- *Card Tricks* by Cynthia Klingel and Robert Noyed. Compass Point Books, 2002.

- *It's Not Magic, It's Science! 50 Science Tricks That Mystify, Dazzle & Astound!* by Hope Buttitta. Lark Books, 2005.

- *Kids' Magic Secrets: Simple Magic Tricks & Why They Work* by Loris Bree. Marlor Press, 2003.

- *Young Magician: Magic Tricks* by Oliver Ho. Sterling Publishing, 2003.

National Roller Skating Month

- *Extreme In-line Skating* by John Crossingham and Bobbie Kalman. Crabtree Publishing Company, 2004.

- *Imaginative Inventions: The Who, What, Where, When, and Why of Roller Skates, Potato Chips, Marbles, and Pie and More!* by Charise Mericle Harper. Little, Brown and Company, 2001.

- *In-line Skating* by Bob Woods. Gareth Stevens, 2004.

- *Sebastian's Roller Skates* by Joan de Deu Prats. Kane/Miller Book Publishers, 2005.

- *Snickerdoodle and the Roller-skating Horse!* by Clare Grosgebauer. Small Wonders Enterprises, 2005.

International Dinosaur Month

Feature your books from 567.9 during International Dinosaur Month, especially these titles:

- *Barnum Brown, Dinosaur Hunter* by David Sheldon. Walker & Co., 2006.

- *Can I Bring My Pterodactyl to School, Ms. Johnson?* by Lois G. Grambling. Charlesbridge, 2006.

- *Did Dinosaurs Eat Pizza? Mysteries Science Hasn't Solved* by Lenny Hort. Henry Holt & Company, 2006.

- *The Extinct Files: My Science Project* by Wallace Edwards. Kids Can Press, 2006.

- *Jurassic Poop: What Dinosaurs (and Others) Left Behind* by Jacob Berkowitz. Kids Can Press, 2006.

October Library and School Events

My Friend Bear

Objectives: To encourage read aloud at home, writing for a purpose, and setting and achieving a class reading goal.

Grades: K–2

General Materials (for each class):

- small stuffed bear

- hard-covered composition notebook (they are often black and white speckled)

- bag to carry notebook and bear

Prepare in Advance:

1. Ask teachers in advance if they are willing to help support the year-long project.

2. Purchase the bears (make sure they can be washed), bags, and notebooks.

3. Get the small canvas bags in the craft section at a discount department store. It should be large enough to hold the stuffed bear and the notebook. On the front, write in pencil "Book Bear on Board." Then trace over it with glitter paint that squeezes through a fine point. Allow to dry. This bag will last for years.

4. Prepare each book so that inside the front cover, the parents will see the parent letter on page 11.

5. The first right-hand page will be the title page that says, "Letters to _____". Insert the bear's name once it has been chosen by the class. Also put the bear's name and the teacher's name on the front cover of the book.

6. The second right-hand page contains a copy of the letter from the class bear that begins "Hello boys and girls," (page 12).

7. The next right-hand page should have the sample student letter (page 13) with the sample picture on the back.

8. Locate the book *My Friend Bear* by Jez Alborough and duplicate a copy of "Fuzzy Wuzzy" and "The Bear Went Over the Mountain" (pages 15–16). Insert the copy in a plastic page protector to keep it handy and easy to store.

Fall Leaves

Whether you have leaf-peeping season in all its splendor, or an overnight leaf drop like we do in Gulf Coast Texas, students can become acquainted with the fall leaves, their shapes, and their colors. Learning to identify trees by their leaves will be a skill children can use their entire life.

Print off copies of the Common Fall Leaves Guide at www.mdc.mo.gov/nathis/seasons/fall/fleaves. It will make the game simpler if you print the leaves in color, though the leaves on the screen won't always be the same color as the guide. Tuck a sheet into a page protector for each computer station you have in the library. Post the address for Leaf Invaders, www.mdc.mo.gov/nathis/seasons/fall/swleaf above each computer. The object of the game is to identify the leaf before it hits the ground from three choices at the bottom of the screen. As students succeed, the leaves fall faster. Students who behave well can use the computers when they complete check out. The game requires Adobe Shockwave, which you will be prompted to load for free if your machine does not have it.

Activity Directions:

1. Before beginning this project, have teacher support and a process for having the students name their bear. We sent ours home with first graders. If you send the bears home with kindergartners, you will have to adjust your letter accordingly so the parent writes the letter dictated by the child and the child draws the picture. Second grade can also do this if you like, but it might be best if it is the privilege of one grade level.

2. Read *My Friend Bear* to the students after a discussion of who has a teddy bear and why they like their favorite one. This book is about a bear with a teddy who meets a boy with a teddy.

3. Afterwards, tell students that this book reminds you of a couple of bear songs that you know. Lead the class in chanting "Fuzzy Wuzzy" and singing "The Bear Went Over the Mountain."

4. Tell the class, "Singing about a bear that went over the mountain reminds me that I have a bear who is eager to go out, too. He doesn't want to go over a mountain. He wants to go home with you and hear some stories at your house!" Introduce the class bear. Name the bear with students' help.

5. Students will take turns taking the bear home each weekend. The goals are:

    a. for the child to read to, or help the bear hear, three stories over the weekend

    b. to write a letter in the class book to tell what was read to the bear and to write one sentence about what the child and the bear did together over the weekend

6. At the beginning of each class, the child gives the bear to you with the book. After your opening ritual, read the passage, ask for any additional details from the child, and keep a running total of the books read. Jot the number in the upper left corner of the letter. The goal at the end of the year could be 50 books.

7. After you read the weekly letter to the class, decide which child will take the bear home the next Friday. Discuss any guidelines you feel are appropriate. I told children they could take the bears anywhere with them as long as they were protective of the bear and remembered to return it on Monday. One of our bears ended up coming back each week with another item of clothing! Over Christmas, the bears all came home with me and my bear, Kippy Joe, to celebrate the holidays and take a bubble bath (in the washer). If desired, you can take the bears home on the first weekend of every month or the last weekend of each six weeks or quarter.

8. A follow-up lesson could include a nonfiction bear book like *Bears: Paws, Claws, and Jaws*. Before reading, ask students how many kinds of bears they think there are and list them where students can see their names before reading. Tell them to listen to see if any bears need to be added. As they hear the name, add the bear. There are eight kinds of bears: brown bears, American black bears, Asian black bears, polar bears, giant pandas, sun bears, sloth bears, and spectacled bears. Make a chart to list what each eats, what it looks like, and where it lives.

Resources:

Bears: Paws, Claws, and Jaws by Adele Richardson. Bridgestone Books, 2001.

My Friend Bear by Jez Alborough. Candlewick Press, 2001, c1998.

Sample letter to parents

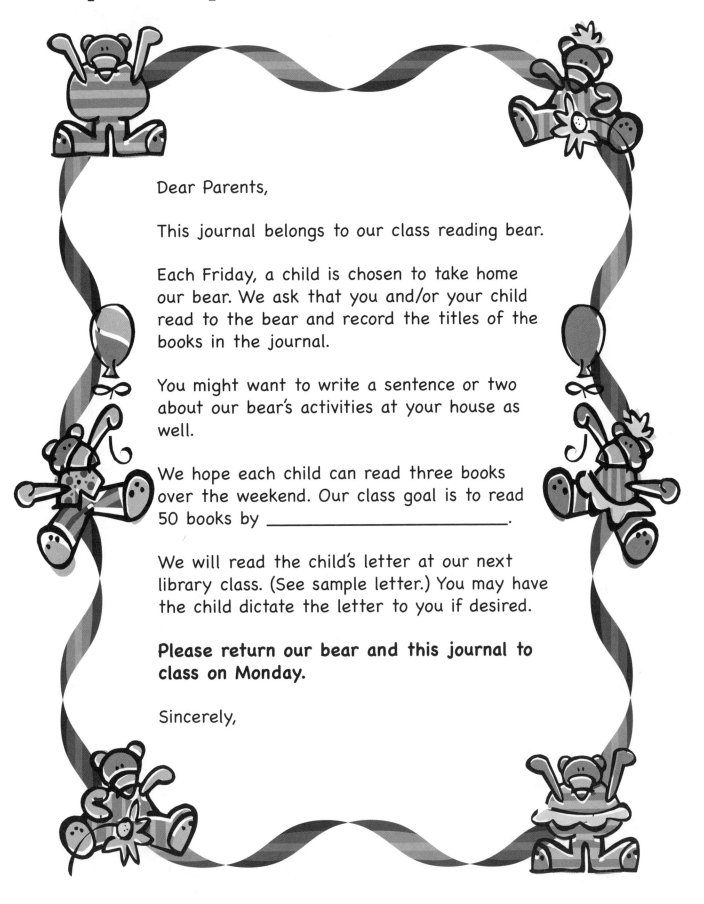

Dear Parents,

This journal belongs to our class reading bear.

Each Friday, a child is chosen to take home our bear. We ask that you and/or your child read to the bear and record the titles of the books in the journal.

You might want to write a sentence or two about our bear's activities at your house as well.

We hope each child can read three books over the weekend. Our class goal is to read 50 books by _____.

We will read the child's letter at our next library class. (See sample letter.) You may have the child dictate the letter to you if desired.

Please return our bear and this journal to class on Monday.

Sincerely,

Hello boys and girls,

I hope you have fun reading to me. Write a letter to list what we read. Can you write down the titles of three books? Then write one thing we did together.

Don't forget to bring me and the journal back on Monday!

Love,

P. S. Please turn the page.

Example of a student letter to the class

Dear Class,

Our bear's name goes here.

This weekend _____

came to my house. Here is what

we read:

1. Corduroy

This is the most important part!

2. Cat in the Hat

3. Rainbow Fish

You can read more than 3.

4. Scruffy

5. Goodnight Moon

We went for a bike ride. Our bear

rode in my back pack.

Tell one thing you did together.

Your friend,

Mike

Don't forget your name!

Example of a student picture

If you'd like, draw a picture of you and our bear on the back of your letter.

Fuzzy Wuzzy

Traditional

Fuzzy Wuzzy was a bear.

Fuzzy Wuzzy had no hair.

If Fuzzy Wuzzy had no hair,

Then Fuzzy Wuzzy wasn't fuzzy,

Was he?

The Bear Went Over the Mountain

(To the tune of "He's a Jolly Good Fellow")

The bear went over the mountain,
The bear went over the mountain,
The bear went over the mountain,
    To see what he could see.

To see what he could see,
To see what he could see,
The bear went over the mountain,
    To see what he could see.

The other side of the mountain,
The other side of the mountain,
The other side of the mountain,
    Was all that he could see.

Was all that he could see,
Was all that he could see,
The other side of the mountain,
    Was all that he could see.

Six Ways to Choose a Book

Objectives: To provide students with a number of ways to find a book when they are overwhelmed by the number of choices, or their own strategies don't work. These methods can be presented over a series of lessons.

Grades: 3–5

Activity Directions:

These are the six strategies. Needed supplies are included with each strategy.

1. **Prize Winner**—Use bookmarks and/or award posters of the Caldecott, Newbery, CSK, and your state award winners to help students know what is available. For state awards, show both past winners and current competitors. Some of the posters are available from book jobbers.

   Show students where the various award books are located if you shelve them separately, and/or any identifying spine labels you might use. Explain to students why the book won, and booktalk a few. For more details and ordering information, go to the American Library Association media award Web site at www.ala.org/Template.cfm?Section=bookmediaawards.

   The state elementary awards for Texas include the Texas 2X2 (age 2 to grade 2) and the Bluebonnet Award. Find the lists and activities at www.txla.org/html/reading.html.

2. **More By an Author**—Compile an ongoing list of your students' favorite authors and post them in alphabetical order along with their call number. Keep each list (F, E, and NF) posted near the proper section of your library. Show students one of your favorite children's authors and all of his/her books you've read. Do a quick talk with opinions of each. Send home a bookmark of authors for children to use at the public library. Post copies at various places in your library. (See page 19.) To guide students to the authors of different genres of fiction, reproduce and distribute the bookmark on page 20.

Carnivorous E-mail

I kept track for a day of where my time was going because I felt I'd accomplished nothing though I'd worked so continuously that I'd skipped lunch.

It was no surprise to find that the biggest consumer of my non-teaching time was my time-eating e-mail. My phone leaves messages on the e-mail as well. Now I only check it first thing in the morning for just 15 minutes, 15 minutes after lunch, and another check 30 minutes before the last bell. The time constraint helps me be judicious in what I read and respond to. Some days it's impossible to stick to those parameters, but not leaving my e-mail open while I'm doing other computer work has been a big time-saver.

3. **Series**—Read aloud a book excerpt from several series and feature them and their location. Make sentence strips with their name and call number and zigzag them down an endcap or bulletin board. For series titles and the books, in order, check out www.mcpl. lib.mo.us/readers /series/juv, provided by the Mid-Continent Public Library. Series provide the comfort and security of known character, plot line, and readability that will be a plus for your less voracious readers.

4. **Genre**—We use genre labels available from Highsmith or Demco to mark our chapter fiction books. We don't mark the realistic fiction books because they make up the largest segment of our collection. But students can find more in their favorite genre by looking for the stickers that indicate mystery, fantasy, science fiction, historical fiction, and suspense (my library's version of horror).

5. **Recommendation by Others**—Students can recommend books to each other, or they can use favorites lists. For some enticing Web sites that recommend books, go to:

Esmé's World: www.planetesme.com/fun.html
This is the site of noted writer and "Readiologist" Esmé Raji Codell, whose enthusiasm will surely win over some of your most reluctant readers. She is the author of a number of children's books as well as *How to Get Your Child to Love Reading: For Ravenous and Reluctant Readers Alike*.

The Book Hive: www.bookhive.org
This is a service of the Public Library of Charlotte & Mecklenburg County. Students can also see and hear professional storytellers Doc McConnell, Tony Tallent, Jackie Torrence, and Donna Washington.

Book Sense: www.booksense.com/bspicks/index.jsp
Bookmark this site before showing students so you can choose one or more of the children's lists by subject or season. Adult books are listed separately.

6. **PAC to Search by Subject**—Be adventuresome! Demonstrate to students how to locate books by subject. Above the PAC computers, create a word wall of favorite subjects, in alphabetical order, so students can refer to them if their own brains can't think of anything they want to read about. Brainstorm with students to create the word list. I like sentence strips that can be cut to length and arranged in order.

The Mighty Pen

I received a letter from a second grader. He wanted to know when AR was going to start. "I want to be more chalengd at reading ..." What a bold step when this child knows things can be accomplished by writing, even if you can't spell all the challenging words.

Authors for K–2

Verna Aardema	Patricia McKissack
Tedd Arnold	Bruce McMillan
José Aruego	David McPhail
Frank Asch	James Marshall
Mary Jane Auch	Bill Martin, Jr.
Molly Bang	Mercer Mayer
Jan Brett	Eve Merriam
Norman Bridwell	Robert Munsch
Larry Dane Brimner	Lynn Munsinger
Marc Brown	Laura Numeroff
Anthony Browne	Kevin O'Malley
Eve Bunting	Mary Pope Osborne
Janell Cannon	Margie Palatini
Nancy Carlson	Peggy Parish
Eric Carle	Barbara Park
Peter Catalanotto	Dav Pilkey
Lynne Cherry	Brian and Jerry Pinkney
Lauren Child	Patricia Polacco
Eileen Christelow	Beatrix Potter
Joanna Cole	Chris Raschka
Donald Crews	Peggy Rathmann
Susan Stevens Crummel	Cynthia Rylant
Demi	Allen Say
Tomie dePaola	April Pulley Sayre
Richard Egielski	Jon Scieszka
Lois Ehlert	Maurice Sendak
Lisa Campbell Ernst	Dr. Seuss
Denise Fleming	David Shannon
Mem Fox	Lane Smith
Gail Gibbons	Eileen Spinelli
Patricia Reilly Giff	William Steig
Ruth Heller	Janet Stevens
Kevin Henkes	Simms Taback
Mary Ann Hoberman	Martin Waddell
Pat Hutchins	Rosemary Wells
Steve Jenkins	Nadine Bernard Westcott
Keiko Kasza	David Wiesner
Holly Keller	Mo Willems
Steven Kellogg	Vera B. Williams
Eric A. Kimmel	Audrey and Don Wood
Loreen Leedy	Jane Yolen
Helen Lester	Ed Young
Arnold Lobel	

Authors for 3–5

David Adler	Lois Lowry
Hans Christian Andersen	David Macaulay
Caroline Arnold	Ann M. Martin
Avi	Jim Murphy
Natalie Babbitt	Marissa Moss
Lynne Reid Banks	Phyllis Reynolds Naylor
Joan Bauer	Barbara Park
Michael Bond	Linda Sue Park
Franklyn M. Branley	Katherine Paterson
Joseph Bruchac	Gary Paulsen
Betsy Byars	Robert Newton Peck
Beverly Cleary	Andrea Davis Pinkney
Ellen Conford	Brian Pinkney
Roald Dahl	Daniel Pinkwater
Paula Danziger	Jack Prelutsky
Leo and Diane Dillon	Rick Riordan
Betsy Duffey	J. K. Rowling
Paul Fleischman	Pam Muñoz Ryan
Sid Fleischman	Louis Sachar
Douglas Florian	Judith St. George
Russell Freedman	Robert D. San Souci
Jean Fritz	Alvin Schwartz
Jack Gantos	Jon Scieszka
Patricia Reilly Giff	Brian Selznick
Paul Goble	Diane Siebert
Jacob and Wilhelm Grimm	Shel Silverstein
Dan Gutman	Seymour Simon
Mary Downing Hahn	Robert Kimmel Smith
Karen Hesse	Lemony Snicket
Carl Hiaasen	Donald J. Sobol
Lee Bennett Hopkins	Jerry Spinelli
James Howe	Mildred D. Taylor
Johanna Hurwitz	Wendelin Van Draanen
Trina Schart Hyman	Vivian Vande Velde
Eric A. Kimmel	Marvin Terban
Dick King-Smith	E. B. White
Rudyard Kipling	Laura Ingalls Wilder
Suzy Kline	David Wisniewski
E. L. Konigsburg	Valerie Worth
Gordon Korman	Betty Ren Wright
Kathleen Krull	Laurence Yep
Kathryn Lasky	Jane Yolen
Patricia Lauber	Harriet Ziefert
Julius Lester	

Choosing a Fiction Book

Give the book 25 pages.
Don't like it? Start another!

Sure Bets

Newbery Winners—chosen by librarians
State Book Awards—chosen by kids

Adventure

Gary Paulsen

Peg Kehret

All Genres

Avi

Humor

Betsy Byars	Johanna Hurwitz
Beverly Cleary	Louis Sachar
Ellen Conford	Jerry Spinelli

Ghost Stories

Betty Ren Wright

Mary Downing Hahn

Realistic

Judy Blume

Lois Lowry

Mystery

Joan Lowery Nixon	Donald Sobol
Geronimo Stilton	

Sports

Alfred Slote

Matt Christopher

Historical Fiction

Pam Conrad	Karen Cushman
Patricia MacLachlan	Mildred Taylor
Laura Ingalls Wilder	

Fantasy

Natalie Babbitt	Susan Cooper
Bruce Coville	Brian Jacques
Dick King-Smith	J. K. Rowling

Choosing a Fiction Book

Give the book 25 pages.
Don't like it? Start another!

Sure Bets

Newbery Winners—chosen by librarians
State Book Awards—chosen by kids

Adventure

Gary Paulsen

Peg Kehret

All Genres

Avi

Humor

Betsy Byars	Johanna Hurwitz
Beverly Cleary	Louis Sachar
Ellen Conford	Jerry Spinelli

Ghost Stories

Betty Ren Wright

Mary Downing Hahn

Realistic

Judy Blume

Lois Lowry

Mystery

Joan Lowery Nixon	Donald Sobol
Geronimo Stilton	

Sports

Alfred Slote

Matt Christopher

Historical Fiction

Pam Conrad	Karen Cushman
Patricia MacLachlan	Mildred Taylor
Laura Ingalls Wilder	

Fantasy

Natalie Babbitt	Susan Cooper
Bruce Coville	Brian Jacques
Dick King-Smith	J. K. Rowling

We Love Our Dogs

Objectives: To share fiction and nonfiction with students through a popular topic, and to use multiple intelligences to engage students in reading.

Grades: K–2

Materials:

- large dog puppet
- pillow for dog
- bone for dog
- *Harry the Dirty Dog* book and plush figure *(optional*—figure can be ordered from Wokits, store.wokits.com/harrydirtydog.html)

Prepare in Advance:

1. Duplicate the songs on pp 26–27 and put them in page protector sleeves.
2. Duplicate the BINGO illustrations on pages 23–25 onto cardstock to spell out B-I-N-G-O.
3. Set the dog on its pillow or in its bed near your chair.
4. Bring a picture of your dog(s) to be displayed in the library.
5. Write a parent letter for each student requesting photos of the family dog (if they have one), explaining the photos will be put up on a bulletin board in the media center.
6. Put the book and plush or other dog clue into the treasure box (optional).

Activity Directions:

1. Use the puppet to sing the chorus, first verse (see modifications), and chorus again of "How Much is That Doggie in the Window." Have the dog puppet chime in at the end of each line. I've included the entire song, but I don't use the verses after the first.

2. After showing the book and the figure, tell students that this book is about a dog who doesn't like to take a bath. How many of them have a dog? How many of their dogs like to take a bath? How many don't? Have students turn to their neighbor and talk about the time they had to give a dog a bath or watch one getting a bath. Allow discussion time.

3. Share the story of *Harry the Dirty Dog*. After the story, show students a picture of your dog. One of mine happens to look a lot like Harry. Tell students that you would love to see their dogs as well, but school rules don't allow dogs to come in the library. However, they can bring a picture of their dog to the library to put on the bulletin board or be displayed. Read the parent letter to them and tell students you will be sending it home with them today.

This is Hank.

Since I have no bulletin board, I've taped page-size cardboard together so I can zigzag it accordion-style on top of the shelves and paperclip their photos to the cardboard. Use the parent letters to attach a sticky note below the photo naming the child and the dog.

4. Before singing about another dog, set out the large cards where each child can see them. Explain how to sing "Bingo." Tell them that each round after the first, you will turn one card so they only see the back. This means they clap the letter. Sing the song slowly the first time through, pointing to each card in turn. Then sing it again a little faster, still pointing to the cards.

Resources:

Harry the Dirty Dog by Gene Zion. HarperCollins, 2002, c1956.

Up and Running

As this year gets off to a running start, I'm reminded of an 18-wheeler. From a complete start, it takes numerous gear shifts, jerky forward motions, smoke, and noise to get the rig going. Once up to speed, it can run so smoothly that another truck can draft in its wake. So far we are jerking through the gears as we adjust to a new challenging schedule, train numerous adult and children volunteers, and get the habits and procedures of the library launched.

The Storytime Treasure Box

Another routine involves setting the stage for the book we are going to share. Before students arrive, I place the book in the bottom of my treasure box and cover it with a fancy gold cloth. On top of the cloth is an item that gives a hint about what the book is about.

The procedure is to select a child (use the library cards and mark with a sticker) to open the box and remove the item. The child shows it to the class and asks for three guesses. She chooses a boy, a girl, and another to guess. Children should respond in complete sentences. After the third guess, tell the class what the relevant magic word is. When we were going to read *My Brother Martin*, I told them the magic word was "Martin Luther King Jr." For *Pip and Squeak*, the magic word was "snowflake." Count to three and the whole class says the word as the host child grabs the magic cloth in the box, and snaps it out with a flourish. If the child has a magical imagination, a book will appear beneath the cloth. If the helper can read the title, let her/him. Show the book to the children and proceed with the lesson.

B

I

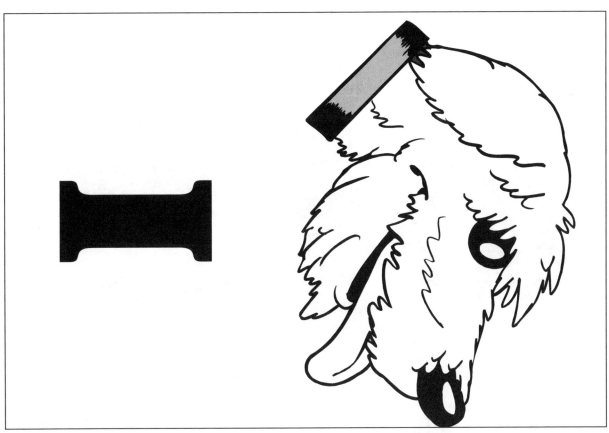

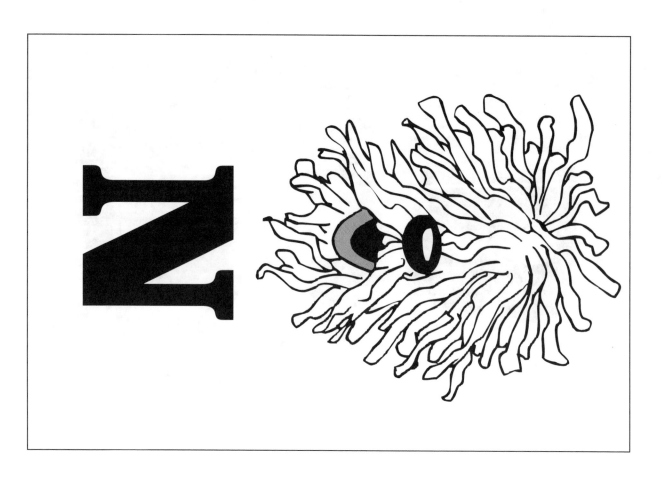

BINGO

Traditional

There was a farmer had a dog,

And BINGO was his name-o!

B-I-N-G-O!

B-I-N-G-O!

B-I-N-G-O!

And Bingo was his name-o!

Now on each verse replace a letter with a clap.

Verse two, for example, would be:

There was a farmer had a dog,

And BINGO was his name-o!

(Clap)-I-N-G-O!

(Clap)-I-N-G-O!

(Clap)-I-N-G-O!

And Bingo was his name-o!

How Much is That Doggie in the Window?

(Bob Merrill, 1952—For music, visit www.niehs.nih.gov/kids/lyrics/howmuch.htm.)

How much is that doggie in the window? *(Arf! Arf!)*
The one with the waggley tail. *(Arf! Arf!)*
How much is that doggie in the window? *(Arf! Arf!)*
I do hope that doggie's for sale. *(Arf! Arf!)*

I must take a trip to California
And leave my poor sweetheart alone.
If he has a dog, he won't be lonesome
And the doggie will have a good home.

(I modify the second and third lines of this verse as:
And leave my poor children alone.
If they have a dog, they won't be lonesome)

How much is that doggie in the window?
The one with the waggley tail.
How much is that doggie in the window?
I do hope that doggie's for sale

I read in the paper there are robbers
With flashlights that shine in the dark.
My love needs a doggie to protect him
And scare them away with one bark.

I don't want a bunny or a kitty.
I don't want a parrot that talks.
I don't want a bowl of little fishies.
He can't take a goldfish for a walk.

How much is that doggie in the window?
The one with the waggley tail.
How much is that doggie in the window?
I do hope that doggie's for sale.
I do hope that doggie's for sale.

Columbus Day from Another View

Objectives: To compare/contrast points of view about Columbus's "mistake" and to explain the origin of Columbus Day.

Grades: 3–5

Materials:

- books about Columbus and his travels to the new world
- books about the new world in the early 1500s
- picture of Christopher Columbus

Prepare in Advance:

Locate a book in your collection that shows what the maps of Columbus's time looked like. When we demonstrate Columbus's voyage on a modern map, it give students the impression that he just went off course. A picture of a map at the time will show students that there was no course to go off of—he was inventing the course, at least for the Spanish. Some good books with these maps are listed in the resource section. A sample, from the Library of Congress, can be seen at www.loc.gov/exhibits/1492/mediterr.html.

Activity Directions:

1. Columbus Day was first celebrated on October 12, 1792, the three hundredth anniversary of the morning when a sailor on the *Pinta* sighted land in what turned out to be the Bahamian island of Guanahani. Sing one of the Columbus songs and talk about songs or rhymes students may have learned in preschool or primary grades (www.preschooleducation.com/scolumbus.shtml). One rhyme students may know is, "In fourteen hundred and ninety two, Columbus sailed the ocean blue." Why do students think Columbus's voyages (he made four) were so important? Divide the class into groups of three to discuss the following

Office Supplies

If you haven't ordered your office supplies and any incentives or prizes you use with students, now is the time to do so. Highsmith, Demco, and Oriental Trading Company are good places for low cost incentives. Does your accounting office allow you to have an open purchase for supplies at a local store? My experience has been that such an arrangement gets the materials to you quicker and at a nice discount. My districts have also been large enough to have a central warehouse for basic supplies. Check with your secretary for a catalog, or find out how to use your online one.

two questions. Give them paper and pencil to jot notes to report back to the class in a time you set.

- What good things came from Columbus' discovery of the New World in the Caribbean?

- What were some negative things?

2. Compile the responses where students can see them. Then tell them that there are other ways to view Columbus and subsequent people in the New World. One of them is the viewpoint of the people who were already on the land and had been for generations. These were the Taino people—named Indians by Columbus who thought he had arrived in India. Why don't we readily know about this event from their side as well? Why don't we sing songs and rhymes from their viewpoint? (They died out, there were few records in their language, they lived on an island so their story didn't spread far, etc.)

3. Author Jane Yolen did research to find out more about the Taino side of the story to write the book *Encounter*. Because few were there to record the story, Jane Yolen had to supply much of it, though she based it on the research she found. This is called historical fiction. Listen for the good and bad that the Taino found in Columbus's visit to their island. (Point out that the book is illustrated beautifully by David Shannon, the man who wrote and illustrated *No, David.*)

4. What do students think were the pros and cons? Was the voyage an overall success or failure? How can they back up their opinion?

Resources:

For more background information and additional activities, see Jamie Huggard's lesson for grades four and five at <u>teacherlink.ed.usu.edu/tlresources/units/Byrnes-celebrations/columbus.html</u>.

Feature your Columbus books in a display. The following include some of the newest research and may have a more balanced viewpoint than some of the older books in your collection.

Christopher Columbus: Explorer of the New World by Peter Chrisp. DK Publishing, 2006.

Christopher Columbus: To the New World by James Lincoln Collier. Marshall Cavendish, 2007.

Columbus and the Age of Explorers by Nadia Higgins. Rourke Press, 2007.

Encounter by Jane Yolen. Harcourt Brace, 1992.

U. S. Suggestion Box

Use an old mailbox as a suggestion box. I spray painted mine gold and set it out next to a container of pencils and a small box of paper slips. Students can suggest books, AR quizzes, programs, authors to visit, and any other thing they can think of to improve the library. When they put in suggestions, they raise the red flag. If suggestions are signed, I reply directly to the child to let him or her know when a suggested book or quiz is in. Some of the things they have suggested include: puppet shows for intermediate grades, add Calvin and Hobbes books, and allow more time to choose books.

Reading the Shelves

Objectives: Students will learn the physical way to look at the shelves to find a book.

Grades: K-2, 3–5

Materials:

- colorful yarn or ribbon

- shelf labels *(Thanks to Barbara Jinkins, Ric Hasenyager, and Donna Sparks for the idea!)*

- six chairs (or two for each shelf that is in your typical book case)

- copies of the two Search sheets on pages 33–34

- transparencies of same two search sheets

- pencils

Prepare in Advance:

K–2 (optional for intermediate grades):

1. Before activity, label shelves with the system you intend to teach to your students.

2. Set up six chairs so they are in a large space. Chairs should face each other across a space of about ten feet. A second pair should be aligned about three feet from the first, etc. These chairs (see diagram) represent the beginning and end of a shelf in a bookcase.

3. Loosely tie a piece of yarn or ribbon to the bottom of two facing chair legs so it lies on the floor. This indicates the width of the shelves.

3–5:

1. Copy the reproducibles for student use. Each pair of students will need a copy of Fiction (and Everybody) (E) Shelving (page 33) and the matching author list (page 36). For a lesson on another day, give student pairs the nonfiction pages on 34 and 37.

2. Make transparencies of the appropriate pages.

3. Set up the overhead projector.

Activity Directions:

K–2:

1. Show students that shelves are "read" in a zigzag fashion when looking for a book. You start at the left of a shelf and proceed to the right (demonstrate). If the book you want is not there, you zig down to the beginning (left) of the next shelf and zag (read) to the right. Repeat the zig and the zag for each shelf until you find the book.

2. Have a Zig Zag March. Be certain the ribbons or yarn are loose enough that they lie on the floor and won't trip students. Line students up at the X on the diagram. Students proceed from the chair on the left to the chair on the right. Sit for a split second in the chair, then zig to the chair in the next row on the left. Subsequent children follow behind, starting for the second chair as the first child starts for the third. When they have zigged and zagged through all six chairs, they should sit in a designated area. Demonstrate again how what we did with chairs is the same way we read the shelves.

3. Explain your library's shelf labels. To help younger students, you may want to label the shelves with pictures and names as well as numbers. Shelf labels follow on pages 38–42. They can be photocopied onto any full-page label sheet and cut out.

3–5:

1. Use the steps above if you want to begin with a kinesthetic exercise to engage your learners.

2. Adapt the next steps to fit your library. Each of my shelves indicates the letters or numbers that begin on that shelf. There is no ending number or letter. I found that students were too confused by the idea of their number or author letters being BETWEEN the ones they saw on the shelf.

3. Instead, the shelf label may say BRE. The one below might say BOT. I teach them to think, "Are my letters after BRE?" If the answer is yes, they look at the label on the next shelf and ask, "Are my letters after BOT?" If the answer is no, they look at the BRE shelf and move from the left to the right. If the answer is yes, proceed to the shelf after the BOT one and ask if the letters come after those, etc. Procedure is similar for the numbers. (Practicing author alphabetical order—with the "Sticks and Stones" game from Upstart, or on pages 9–13 of *Stretchy Library Lessons: Research Skills*—has been a big help to my students in ordering author names to the third letter.)

4. To practice this concept as a group before moving to the shelf, make a transparency of your shelf configuration. Page 33 works for my shelves because they are constructed as described above. If you use a different system, configure your transparency on page 35 to match. Explain the page to students and tell them we are going to practice locating books on paper, and then we will go to shelves and locate them for real. After explaining the labeling on the "shelves" have students look at Case 1. On which shelves would the books be whose author starts with B? with H? Ask similar questions for Case 2 and 3.

5. Ask students to look at Case 1 and the "books" listed by author on page 36 for Case 1. Which of those books would go on the shelf labeled A? Have students confer and answer. Discuss their decision. Proceed with shelf D in the same manner. Then shelf G. If there is time do the same with Case 2 and Case 3.

6. In another lesson, help students to "shelve" the nonfiction "books" on page 37 into the cases on page 35.

Fiction Answers:

Case 1:
On the A shelf: Janet Ahlberg, Jan Brett, Karen Cushman
On the D shelf: Roald Dahl, Ian Falconer,
On the G shelf: James Cross Giblin, Eric Hill, Susan Jeffers, Pat Miller

Case 2:
On BRE shelf: Marc Brown, Alexandra Day, Lisa Ernst
On FAL shelf: Mem Fox, Sherry Garland, Ruth Heller
On HON shelf: Lily Hong, James Howe, Ezra Jack Keats
Case 3:
On PAC shelf: Gary Paulsen, Katherine Paterson
On PAX shelf: Tom Paxton, Bill Peet, Dav Pilkey, Jerry Pinkney
On POE shelf: Jack Prelutsky, Patricia Polacco, Robin Pulver

Nonfiction Answers:

Case 1:
Ask on which shelf these numbers would be: 3, 17, 20, 7, 1, 8, 14, 5. The answers would be 1, 15, 15, 6, 1, 6, 6, 1—the numbers that begin the shelf.

Case 2:

| 500: 508, 523, 540 | 550: 51.5, 570, 579 | 580: 581, 599.3, 587 |

Case 3:

| 618: 620, 632, 650, 645.7 | 654: 658, 682 | 683: 684.1, 698, 685 |

Fiction (and Everybody) Shelving

Case 1

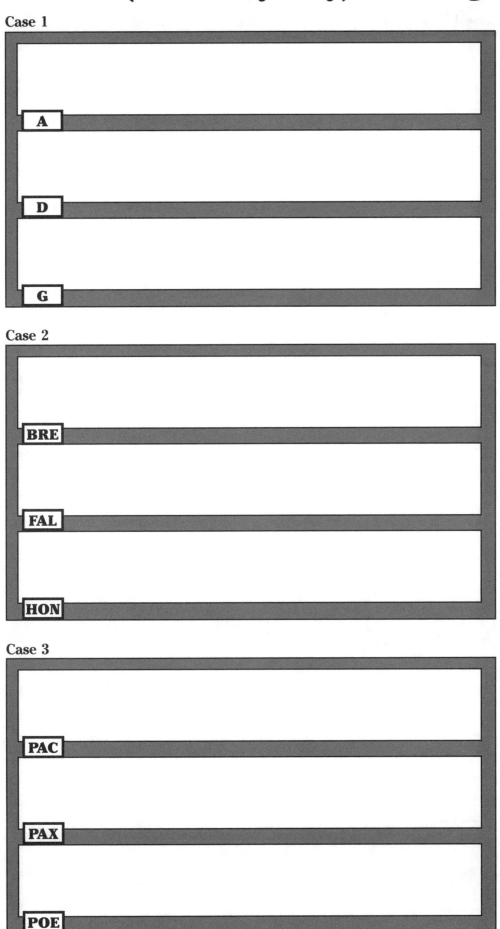

A

D

G

Case 2

BRE

FAL

HON

Case 3

PAC

PAX

POE

Nonfiction Shelving

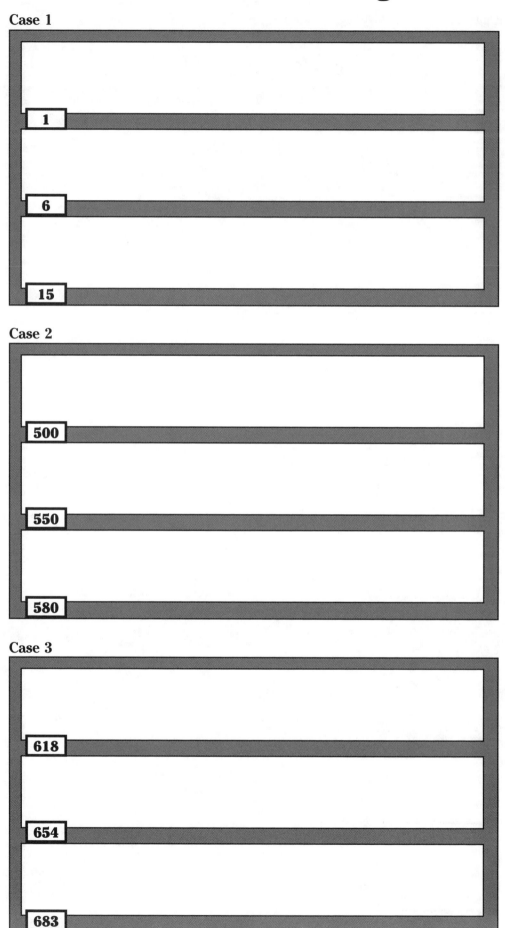

Case 1

1

6

15

Case 2

500

550

580

Case 3

618

654

683

Nonfiction Shelving

Case 1

Case 2

Case 3

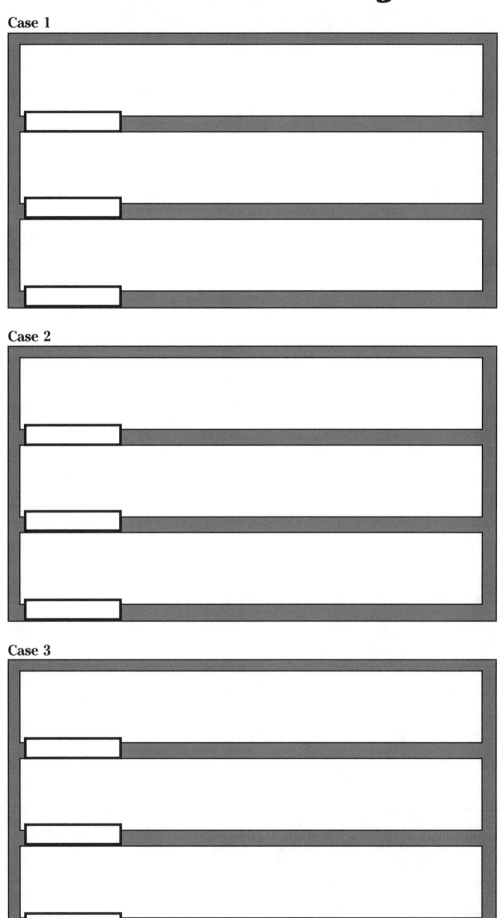

Fiction (and Everybody) Shelving

For the first case, ask which shelf, A, D, or G the following names would be located. Remember to use author's last name.

Case 1

Janet Ahlberg	Jan Brett	Eric Hill
Roald Dahl	Ian Falconer	James Cross Giblin
Susan Jeffers	Pat Miller	Karen Cushman

Case 2

Mem Fox	Marc Brown	Sherry Garland
Lisa Ernst	Ruth Heller	Ezra Jack Keats
Lily Hong	Alexandra Day	James Howe

Case 3

Dav Pilkey	Tom Paxton	Gary Paulsen
Jerry Pinkney	Jack Prelutsky	Patricia Polacco
Bill Peet	Katherine Paterson	Robin Pulver

Nonfiction

Case 2

508	551.5	581
540	570	579
599.3	587	523

Case 3

684.1	658	620
698	645.7	650
632	685	682

Dewey Shelf Labels

031 Guinness World Records	**133.1** Ghosts
200 Religions	**292** Mythology
324.6 Elections	**328.73** U.S. Government
359 Military	**393.3** Mummies
394.2 Holidays	**398.2** Fairy Tales
398.2 Folktales	**398.8** Mother Goose
400 Language	**430** German
440 French	**460** Spanish
490 Other Languages	**500** Math
523 Stars	 **523.4** Planets

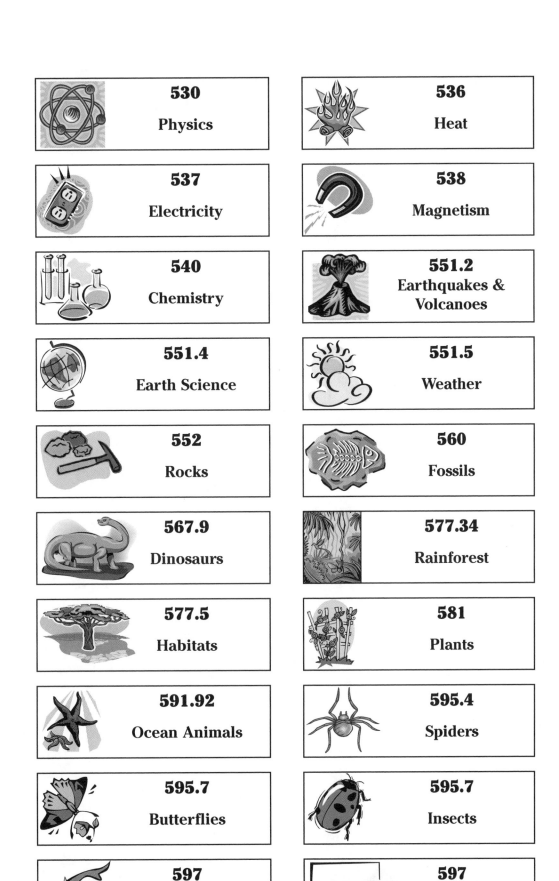

530
Physics

536
Heat

537
Electricity

538
Magnetism

540
Chemistry

551.2
Earthquakes &
Volcanoes

551.4
Earth Science

551.5
Weather

552
Rocks

560
Fossils

567.9
Dinosaurs

577.34
Rainforest

577.5
Habitats

581
Plants

591.92
Ocean Animals

595.4
Spiders

595.7
Butterflies

595.7
Insects

597
Sharks

597
Fishes

597.6
Amphibians

 **597.8**
Frogs

 597.9
Reptiles

 597.96
Snakes

 **598**
Birds

 599
Mammals

 **599.75**
Big Cats

 608
Inventions

 610
Health

 612
Human Body

 612.8
Senses

 613
Foods

 **629.133**
Airplanes

 **629.222**
Automobiles

 629.228
Race Cars

 629.4
Space Travel

 630
Farming

 634
Apples

 635
Pumpkins

 635
Gardening

 **636**
Farm Animals

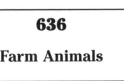 **636**
Pets

636.1
Horses

 636.7
Dogs

636.8
Cats

 641.5
Cookbooks

736
Origami

 741
Drawing

741.5
Dance

 741.5
Graphic Novels

745.5
Crafts

 780
Music

 791.6
Cheerleading

 793.73
I Spy

 **793.8**
Magic

 796
Sports

 796.323
Basketball

 796.332
Football

 796.334
Soccer

 796.357
Baseball

808

Jokes & Riddles

 **811**

Poetry

 912

Atlases

 **932**

Ancient Egypt

 940

Wars

 940.3

World War I

 940.54

World War II

 944

Europe

 951

Asia

 960

Africa

 970

North America

 973.7

Civil War

 980

South America

 994

Australia

Publisher Assigned Reading Levels

In beginning reader books, often called "step-up" books, publishers do not agree on what constitutes a Level One, Two, Three, or Four book. Set your own standards for uniformity if you display books by step-up level. Re-label those that are too high for your criteria. Here is mine:

Step 1: Very large print, lots of white space, beginning words, few words per page, sometimes has rebus pages. Examples:

- (My First Hello Reader with Flash Cards) *I See a Bug*

- (Step Into Reading: Ready to Read) *I Like Bugs*

Step 2: Large font, more words per page, can perhaps be read with help. Examples:

- (Step Into Reading: Reading with Help) *P. J. Funnybunny Bag of Tricks*

- (Hello Reader 2) *Two Crazy Pigs*

Step 3: Beginning to approximate typical book font, more text per page, smaller illustrations, more complex plot. Example:

- (Step Into Reading: Reading on Your Own) *Happy Valentine's Day, Miss Hildy.*

Step 4: Often has chapter divisions and titles, beginning chapter books that have an easier vocabulary. Examples:

- Frog and Toad series

- Nate the Great series

- (Road to Reading: First Chapters) *The Stone Giant: The Hoax That Fooled America*

- Young Cam Jansen series

Reading Incentive Ideas

Short, frequent reading programs are often more successful than a year-long program. The more varied each one is, the more likely you are to eventually appeal to every reader, even the passive ones. Here are some that I have used:

Texas Reading Club (Substitute your mascot, name, or state.)

Children must read five fiction, four nonfiction, and one medal-winner to earn the certificate and prize for the Texas Reading Club. It could last for just one semester or one quarter. The nonfiction have to be one science, one history, one biography, and one free choice NF book. The medal-winner can be Caldecott, Newbery, CSK, or your state award book. Supply students with a bookmark of the winners or display posters.

Completion of the 10 books, ascertained by the teacher through reporting of some kind of AR or RC quiz earns the student a free book from my collection or a free book from the next Scholastic Book Club flyer. Because I use the monthly flyers to order paperbacks for the library, I use bonus points to get books without charge. Use "My Reading Record" on page 45 to help students keep track. Use the transparency master on the following page to show students how to record their reading. (The example on page 46 included books I had read at the time.) A dash in the last column indicates a book I began but didn't like. I tell students to give a book 20–25 pages before quitting it.

Olympic Reading

Go to www.highsmith.com/webapp/wcs/stores/servlet/Production/LSP/pages/2004_pdfs/lsp_aug_olympics.pdf for nineteen pages of activities and forms you will need to host the Reading Olympics at your school. Set a goal with students to read so many pages, books, or points to earn their Olympic medals. (Order from Demco.) Have a ceremony complete with music during which you award the medals. We used "Gonna Fly Now," the theme from the movie *Rocky*.

Sail the Reading Ocean with Columbus

Make a bulletin board with paper waves stapled at the bottom to form a long pocket across the board, one wave for each grade. Give each class the ship pattern on page 47. The teacher should have a student color it, cut it out, and return it to the library along with the name of their ship. The ship's name would be something like Miller's Marvels or Miller's Mighty Readers. Use a permanent market to write the name along the top board of each ship.

Laminate the ship in such a way that a lot of clear film is left around the ship. Tape the laminated ship to the bottle template on page 48. Cut out the bottle through the plastic so it will look like the ship is in a glass bottle. Add a small piece of brown paper to the neck to look like a cork. "Throw" into the ocean at the left and hope it can float to the far right by a pre-determined day so everyone in the class can check out an extra book or the teacher gets a free book for her/his class or other prize. You can determine the kinds of books, number of books, amount of points, etc., that each class must achieve to cross the ocean. Mark the waves to correspond to steps towards the goal you have set and move the ships-in-a-bottle closer to the end each week.

My Reading Record

Date	F/NF	Genre	Title	Pages	Rating

A dash in the rating column is for books that you didn't finish. For these books, record how many pages you read before quitting.

My Reading Record

Date	F/NF	Genre	Title	Pages	Rating
9/18	F	Realistic	Phoenix Rising	182	A
9/31	F	Realistic	When Zacharay Beaver Came to Town	227	B
10/14	NF	History	Boss of the Plains	32	B
10/16	F	Fantasy	Seven Songs of Merlin	30	—
10/20	NF	Biography	Conversations with J. K. Rowling	96	B
10/30	NF	History	So You Want to Be President?	52	A

A dash in the rating column is for books that you didn't finish. For these books, record how many pages you read before quitting.

Ship pattern for Sail the Reading Ocean with Columbus

Bottle pattern for Sail the Reading Ocean with Columbus

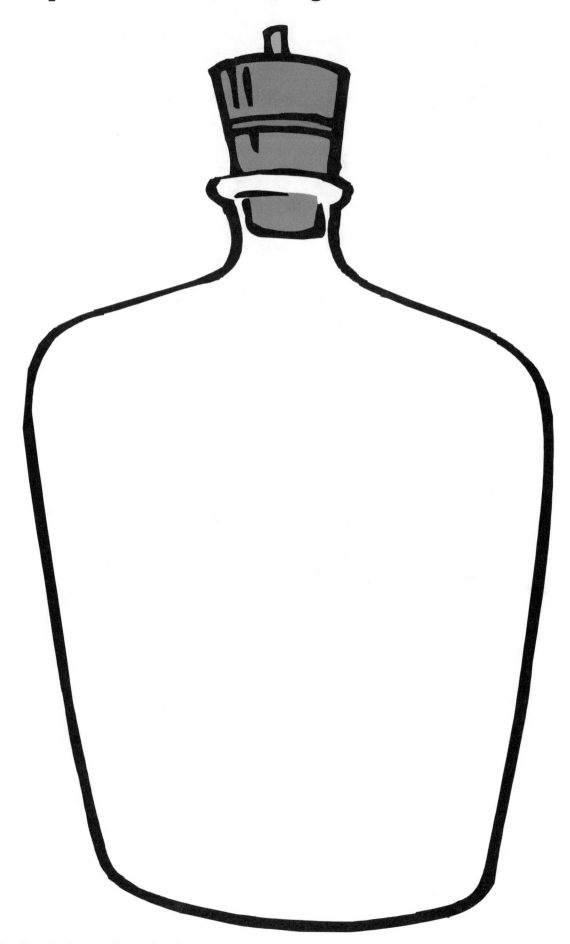

Dancing Bones

Objectives: To share some slightly scary literature for Halloween while reviewing information about the skeletal system.

Grades: K–2, 3–5

Materials:

- bones with statements

- books (K: *Shake Dem Halloween Bones,* 1–2: *Dem Bones,* 3–5: *The Dancing Skeleton*)

- skeleton made to go on flannel board or magnetic board (see pattern on page 59)

- a plastic skeleton from the party or craft store

Prepare in Advance:

1. Duplicate the statements on pages 54–58 on card stock, cut out, and laminate.

2. Make a transparency of the skeleton and project it on sheets of fun foam to enlarge and trace the bones. You will need two complete skeletons for play by two teams. Attach a piece of magnetic tape or Velcro™ to the back of each bone.

3. Set up your flannelboard.

4. Purchase a plastic skeleton or find a large poster of one.

5. Locate the books listed above.

Activity Directions:

Grade K:

1. Ask students if they know the three main purposes of their skeleton (protect organs, give shape to body, help them move). How can they make their skeletons even stronger? (Exercise, drink milk, and eat healthy foods.)

Shadow Puppets

For a spooky presentation of a story, make the book characters from fun foam or heavy cardboard. Open a paper clip at a right angle so one loop can be taped to the figure and the other, bent at a right angle, can be taped to a wooden skewer, pencil, or craft stick.

Make your screen from opaque muslin stretched over a canvas stretcher (available in any store that sells frames) and tacked with staple gun or thumb tacks to the back. Stand the frame by sandwiching it between a pair of book ends on both sides, and attach two clip lamps to the top. Or you can point two gooseneck lamps toward the back of the muslin. Check for shadow quality before performing.

Record yourself reading the story, or have a teacher read the story as you perform it. Put a tablecloth on the table that comes to the floor in front. Put your stage on top with your characters laid out behind it. Seat yourself behind the stage and press the figures against the muslin screen from the back as they are onstage during the reading. A favorite of mine and my students is *Bony Legs* by Joanna Cole. I purchased the story on tape from Scholastic.

2. Share the book *Dem Bones* with students to acquaint them with how their bones are put together. Have them touch their bones as you show them on the skeleton figure or poster.

3. Tell students they will use their personal skeletons to help them play a skeleton game. Their skull will protect their <u>brains</u> which will think about how to play, their <u>eyes</u> that will examine the bones to find the right one, and their <u>tongues</u> which they will use to speak to their group as they play. Their skeleton will help them raise their <u>hand</u> to participate, and to pick up the pieces of the game. Then their skeleton will help them <u>move</u> to show their correct game pieces.

4. The object of the game is to build a skeleton as quickly as they can in front of the group. You can play this like a relay race, or more sedately by having teams take turns placing the bone. Display a plastic skeleton or poster for reference. Each team will have a set of the fun foam bones and a place to adhere them. They will begin with the skull and attach the bones down to the feet bones. If played as a relay, the first team completely done gets to check out an extra book. If played in turn, the team with the most correct bones placed, wins the same privilege. Or give out stickers—fall leaves, pumpkins and skeleton stickers are readily available this time of year.

Grades 1–2:

1. Ask students if they know the three main purposes of their skeleton (protect organs, give shape to body, help them move). How can they make their skeletons even stronger? (Exercise, drink milk, eat healthy foods.)

2. Review the bones by using the skeleton on page 59 to familiarize them with each and its use.

3. Tell students they will use their personal skeletons to help them play a skeleton game. Their skull will protect their <u>brains</u> which will think about how to play, their <u>eyes</u> that will examine the bones to find the right one, and their <u>tongues</u> which they will use to speak to their group as they play. Their skeleton will help them to raise their <u>hand</u> to participate and pick up the pieces of the game. Then their skeleton will help them <u>move</u> to show their correct game pieces.

4. The object of the game is to build a skeleton as quickly as they can in front of the group. You can play this like a relay race, or more sedately by having teams take turns placing the bone. Display a plastic skeleton or poster for reference. Each team will have a set of the fun foam bones and a space on the floor to correctly lay them out. They will begin with the skull and attach the bones down to the feet bones. If played as a relay, the first team completely done gets to check out an extra book. If played in turn, the team with the most correct bones placed, wins the same privilege. Or give out stickers—fall leaves, pumpkins and skeleton stickers are readily available this time of year.

5. End by reading the rap fairy tale version called *Shake Dem Halloween Bones*. Have students use their own strong bones to act out the chorus.

Grades 3–5:

1. Ask students if they know the three main purposes of their skeleton (protect organs, give shape to body, help them move). How can they make their skeletons even stronger? (Exercise, drink milk, eat healthy foods.)

2. Divide the class into two groups and give each the skeleton bones. They must correctly decide on a statement's veracity in order to put a bone on the skeleton. (Assemble team

skeletons on the floor.) First team finished wins. Use the statements on the bones cut out from pages 54–58. Students use the bones in their thumbs to indicate <u>thumbs</u> up for true, thumbs down for false. The entire team must agree on the answer before you can verify it for them. Then choose a student to put the bone down, beginning with the skull.

3. End by reading the spooky folk tale *The Dancing Skeleton.* Be sure to be seated near the skeleton as you read. Even better, seat it in a rocking chair near you!

Resources:

The Dancing Skeleton by Cynthia DeFelice. Aladdin Paperbacks, 1996, 1989.

Dem Bones by Bob Barner. Chronicle Books, 1996.

Shake Dem Halloween Bones by W. Nikola-Lisa. Houghton Mifflin, 1997.

Wiggle Poem

One routine we have is beginning the primary classes with a Wiggle Poem. We act out each line, stretching and reaching on the high and low lines (which we do in our squeaky high and hilarious low voices), and echoing all the rest as we teach the poem to our newest children.

> Sometimes my hands are by my side,
> Then behind my back they hide.
> Shake them fast,
> Shake them slow,
> Shake them high,
> Shake them low.
>
> Sometimes my hands go clap, clap, clap;
> Then I lay them in my lap.
> Now they're quiet as can be.
> Shhh! It's story time you see!
> —*Adapted from an anonymous poem.*

For variety and extra fun, we say the poem lickety split, with a Texas twang, in a mouse voice, or like a tired turtle with corresponding speed or voice inflections.

Each week two students come to the front to help lead the poem. For their service, they get a glittery hand sticker on their library card. The student who opens the treasure box (selected from the library cards) gets a large gold sticker on his/her card.

This form entitles you to check out one extra book today!

This form entitles you to check out one extra book today!

Skeletons: True or False
Answer Key

1. A baby's skull is not solid. *True.*

2. The smallest bone in your body is inside your ear. *True.*

3. Fingernails are made from the same material as bones. *False. Nails are keratin. Bones are calcium.*

4. Fruit juice helps bones get stronger. *False. Milk does.*

5. Bones can repair themselves. *True.*

6. The tailbone is the last bone in your spine. *True.*

7. An example of a ball and socket joint is your elbow. *False. Hip, shoulder.*

8. An example of a swivel joint is your wrist. *True.*

9. An example of a hinge joint is your ankle. *False. Knee, elbow.*

10. The separate bones of your backbone are called phalanges. *False. Vertebrae.*

11. Pelvis is the scientific name for your hip bones. *True.*

12. Cranium is the scientific name for your skull. *True.*

13. Patella is the scientific name for your kneecap. *True.*

14. Your nose is made of two small bones. *False. Cartilage only.*

15. The longest bone in your body is the bone from your shoulder to your wrist. *False. Hip to knee.*

16. Three flexible bones protect your abdomen. *False. Zero.*

17. Blood is produced inside your bones. *True.*

18. An infant has more bones than an adult. *True.*

19. The soft material inside bone is called cartilage. *False. Marrow.*

20. An adult has 246 bones. *False. 206.*

21. Ribs are the bones that protect the heart. *True.*

22. Phalanges is the scientific name for toes and fingers. *True.*

23. Your backbone is made of long, flexible bones. *False. Small, stacked bones.*

24. Your sternum is your skull. *False. Breastbone.*

25. Animal skeletons have the same jobs as human skeletons. *True.*

26. While you are alive, your bones are alive. *True.*

Skeletons: True or False questions

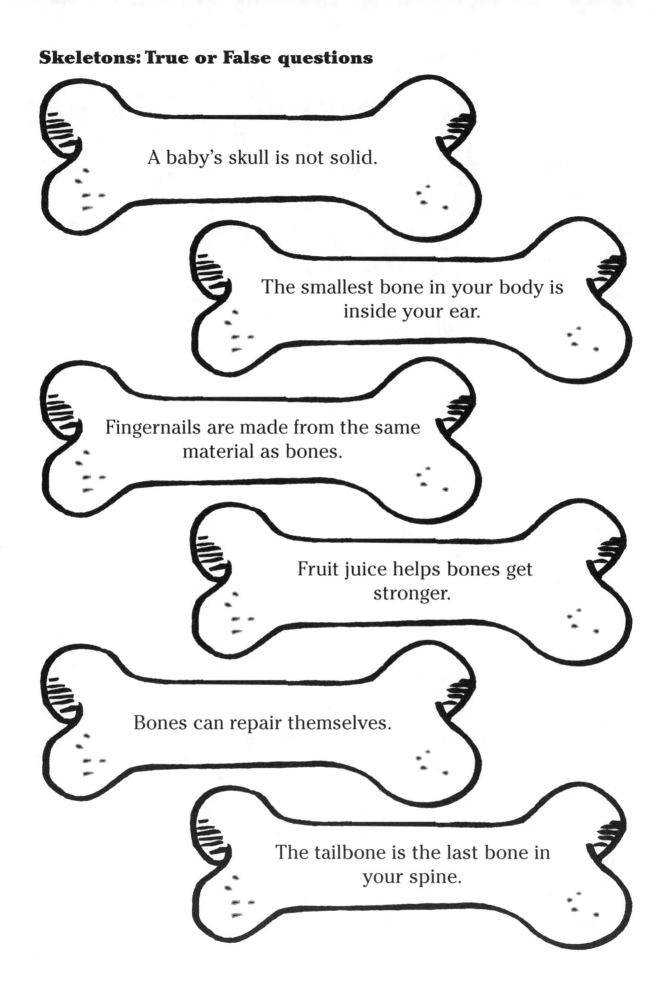

A baby's skull is not solid.

The smallest bone in your body is inside your ear.

Fingernails are made from the same material as bones.

Fruit juice helps bones get stronger.

Bones can repair themselves.

The tailbone is the last bone in your spine.

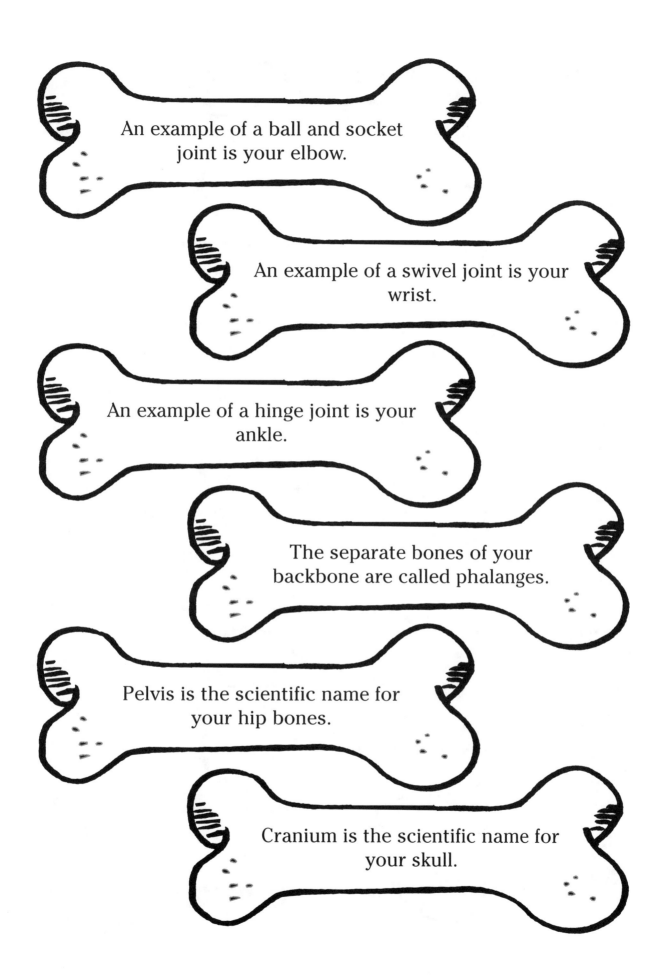

An example of a ball and socket joint is your elbow.

An example of a swivel joint is your wrist.

An example of a hinge joint is your ankle.

The separate bones of your backbone are called phalanges.

Pelvis is the scientific name for your hip bones.

Cranium is the scientific name for your skull.

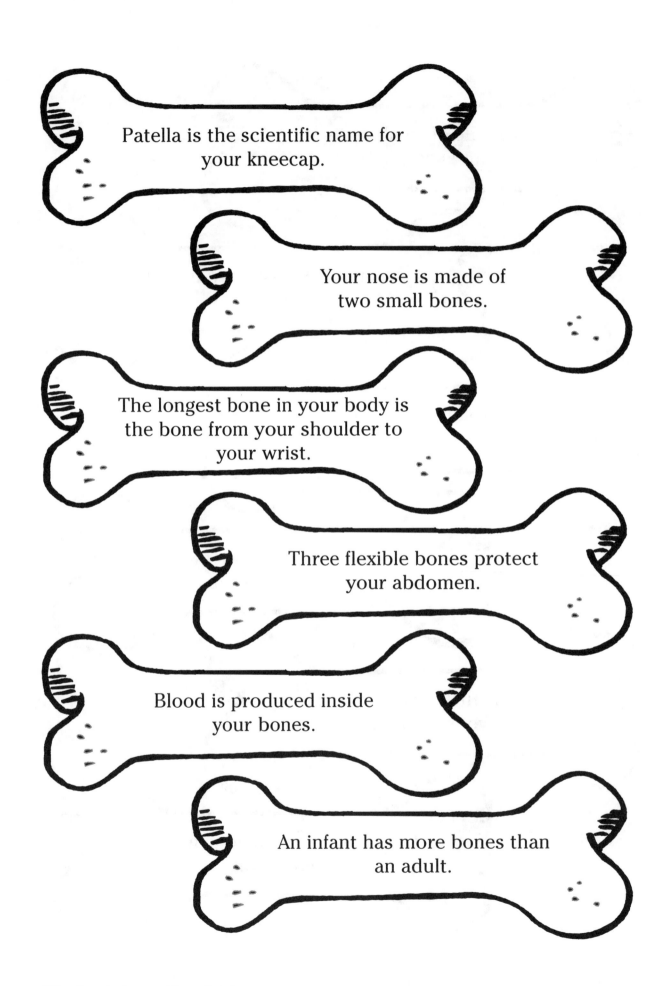

Patella is the scientific name for your kneecap.

Your nose is made of two small bones.

The longest bone in your body is the bone from your shoulder to your wrist.

Three flexible bones protect your abdomen.

Blood is produced inside your bones.

An infant has more bones than an adult.

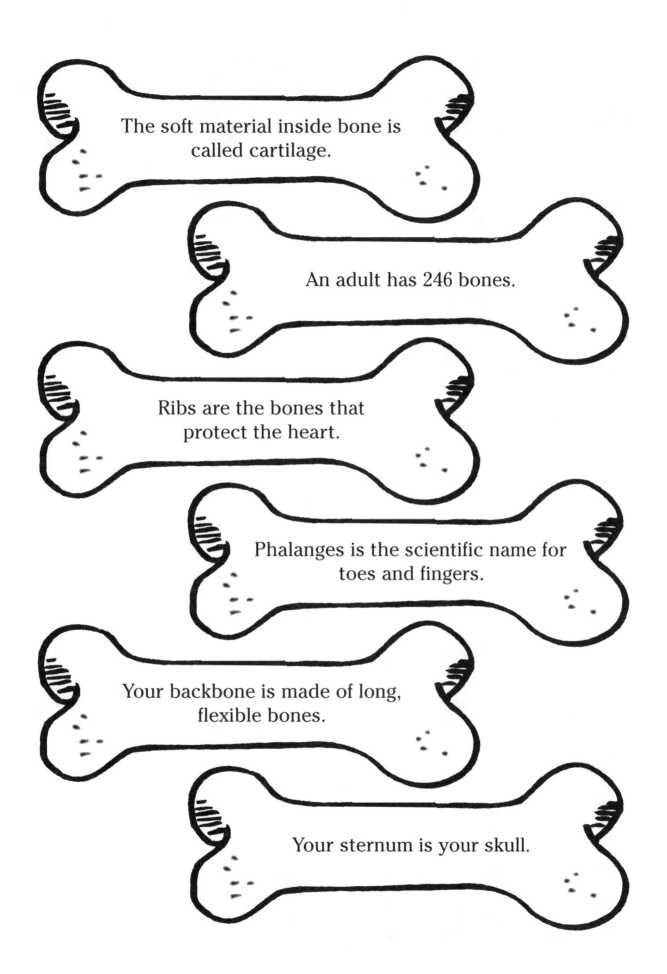

The soft material inside bone is called cartilage.

An adult has 246 bones.

Ribs are the bones that protect the heart.

Phalanges is the scientific name for toes and fingers.

Your backbone is made of long, flexible bones.

Your sternum is your skull.

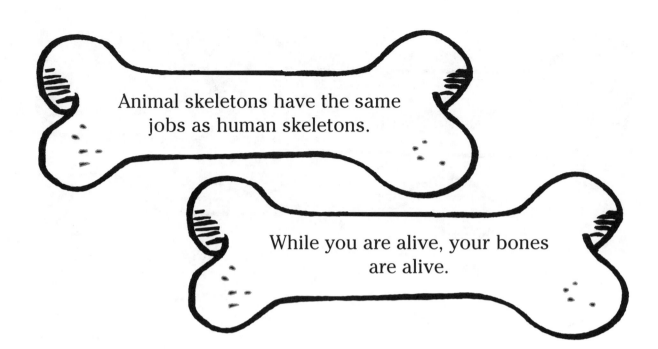

Animal skeletons have the same jobs as human skeletons.

While you are alive, your bones are alive.

Skeleton pattern

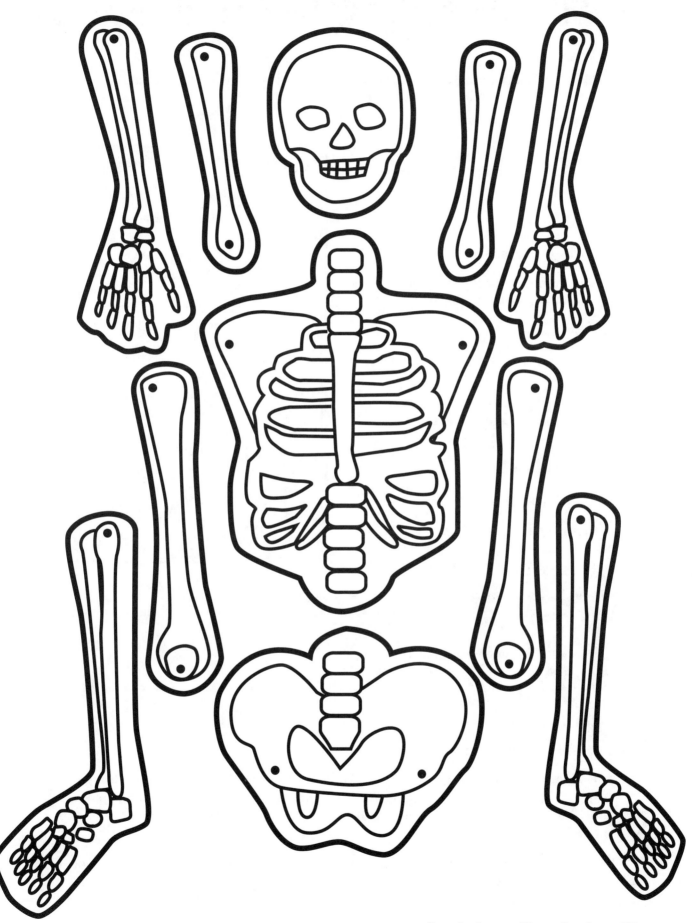

The Pumpkin Fairy

Objectives: To learn about the life cycle of a pumpkin, the power of imagination.

Grades: K–2

Materials:

- small paper cup like the kind ketchup is dispensed into

- pumpkin seed

- six-inch square of muslin

- die-cut green leaf or four-inch green square of construction paper

- very small pumpkin

- several bottles that spray a fine mist

- glitter

- a letter from the pumpkin fairy (reproducible on page 64)

- one large pumpkin

Prepare in Advance:

1. Gather needed materials, including enough cups, seeds, muslin squares, leaves and small pumpkins for each child.

2. Die-cut leaves or green squares and cut the muslin into 6" squares.

3. Duplicate the pumpkin fairy letter.

4. Gather all your books on pumpkins: fiction and nonfiction.

5. Make a tent sign (pattern on page 62) for each teacher in the grade you will do this with. The signs will identify the pumpkin patch on each table. Cover the tables with table-cloths if desired.

Make Your Own Pumpkin Patch

Decorate your library with collapsible pumpkins you and your students make. For each pumpkin, you will need 18 strips of laminated orange construction paper, 1" x 9", two brads, and two leaf shapes. Punch small holes in each strip, ½" from each end. Stack the strips together and insert brad. Add the two leaves to one end before spreading the brad open. Make a pumpkin by spreading the strips out into a globular shape. For larger pumpkins, cut strips that are 1" x 12". For smaller ones, cut 1" x 6" strips. The pumpkins are easy to make and even easier to store.

Activity Directions:

1. This activity is based on an idea my kindergarten teachers and I implement. It takes two weeks. During the first week, the teachers talk about the life cycle of a pumpkin, read books aloud each day, and review the life cycle from seed to blooming plant, to pumpkin, to seed, and repeat.

2. During the first week, students are told that they will use the library like a greenhouse to see if they can grow pumpkins from seed even though it is not spring. They will water the seeds each day and cover them to keep them warm. They draw two lines on their

muslin squares to divide it into four squares. In one they draw a seed. In the second they draw a vine and leaf. In the third (clockwise) they draw a pumpkin flower, in the fourth the small pumpkin (without a face!). That will bring them back to the square with the seed. This is the "blanket" that will cover the seed.

3. Next, students write their names on the outside edge of the leaf or green square and glue their cup in the center of the paper. Allow time to dry.

4. On Monday of the second week, teachers give each student a seed from a pumpkin they scoop out in class. Students put their seeds in their cups. The students bring their cups to the library to arrange on tables with a sign that says, "Ms. _____'s Pumpkin Patch." Have a large pumpkin displayed prominently. Students write to the Pumpkin Fairy.

5. Each day, students come to the library to mist their pumpkin seeds with water. Allow each child to have one squirt. On the morning of the last day before students arrive, replace each seed with a small pumpkin that squashes the cup down flat! Cover with the blankets. Cut a door in the large pumpkin and leave the letter, rolled up and tied with a pretty ribbon, protruding from the door. Leave a glitter trail (this is the path of the pumpkin fairy) from the pumpkin to the tables, and then out a nearby window or door-way or even to a pumpkin book.

6. Classes come to water their seeds and are surprised to find pumpkins instead. Wait til someone notices the letter, read it aloud, and have the children take their pumpkins to class with them for more activities. Re-roll the letter and reinsert for the next class.

Resources:

Nonfiction

A Day at the Pumpkin Patch by Megan Faulkner. Scholastic Canada, 2006.

From Seed to Pumpkin by Jan Kottke. Children's Press, 2000.

From Seed to Pumpkin by Wendy Pfeffer. HarperCollins, 2004.

It's a Fruit, It's a Vegetable, It's a Pumpkin by Allan Fowler. Children's Press, 1995.

Life Cycle of a Pumpkin by Ron Fridell and Patricia Walsh. Heinemann Library, 2001.

Picking Apples & Pumpkins by Amy and Richard Hutchings. Scholastic, 1994.

Pumpkin by Barrie Watts. Smart Apple Media, 2003.

Pumpkin Circle: The Story of a Garden by George Levenson. Tricycle Press, 2002, c1999.

The Pumpkin Patch by Elizabeth King. Puffin, 1996, c1990.

Pumpkins by Jacqueline Farmer. Charlesbridge Publishing, 2004.

Pumpkins by Ken Robbins. Roaring Brook Press, 2006.

Fiction

The Biggest Pumpkin Ever by Steven Kroll. Scholastic, 1984.

Five Little Pumpkins by Iris Van Rynbach. Boyds Mills Press, 2003, c1995.

It's Pumpkin Time! by Zoe Hall. Blue Sky Press, 1999, c1994.

The Littlest Pumpkin by R. A. Herman. Scholastic, 2001.

My Pumpkin by Julia Noonan. Children's Press, 2005.

Pumpkin Day! by Nancy Elizabeth Wallace. Marshall Cavendish, 2002.

The Pumpkin Patch by Margaret McNamara. Aladdin Paperbacks, 2003

Pumpkin, Pumpkin by Jeanne Titherington. Greenwillow Books, 1986.

_____'s

Pumpkin

Patch

Garden of Readin'

Our kindergartners found it difficult to make good choices when faced with thousands of book spines. So I adopted the same book display method teachers use in the classroom, and which is advocated by Jim Trelease, reading expert and author.

I purchased 40 sturdy plastic tubs and placed them so the longest side was now the width Now each bookcase holds four tubs. The first four are numbered 1–4 for our Step Books. Step One is for our newest beginners and Step Four is easier chapter books. The next 20 tubs are labeled with the alphabet letters (pair- or triple-up some of the letters like E/F, U/V/W, etc.). We have one tub labeled "Clifford" and another "Arthur" because we have so many of these books. The last 12 are for nonfiction and are labeled: Farm Animals and Pets, Wild Animals, Ocean Life, Holidays, Math, People, Poetry, Places and Things, Plants, Insects, Magic School Bus, Holidays. The books are labeled NF 1 (for nonfiction tub 1, etc.). The fiction books are simply labeled with the first letter of the author's last name. Use very small labels in the upper left corner of fiction and upper right of the nonfiction.

You might also label tubs: Fairy Tales, Henry and Mudge, Song Books, and ABC Books.

Dear Boys and Girls,

Thank you for taking such good care of your pumpkin seeds.

I have to tell you that anyone can stick a pumpkin seed in the soil. Then the seed does all the work.

But you are very special, because you were willing to grow a pumpkin with your imagination. Your minds did all the work.

Your wishes and your wonderful notes and the pictures you made in your mind—that can make some amazing things happen.

It would not surprise me if many of you can even see me, the Pumpkin Fairy, in your imagination.

Best wishes from your friend,

The Pumpkin Fairy

Seasonal Scripted Reading

Objectives: To perform a piece of literature that coordinates with this time of year.

Grades: 3–5

Materials:

- copies of *Ghost-eye Tree* OR *The Hallo-wiener*

- Reader's Theater scripts for *Hallo-wiener* (www.readinglady.com/downloads/read-erstheater/hallowiener.pdf) or *Ghost-eye Tree* (www.michigan.gov/documents/ReadersTheatreScript_32737_7.pdf)

Prepare in Advance:

1. Duplicate either or both of these scripts. Make 25 copies of *Ghost-eye Tree.* You will only need 14 copies of *The Hallo-wiener* (for 12 readers, one for you and one for the teacher). Put them into pocket folders with brads (even better if they have page protectors) if they have page protectors. This makes for reusable Reader's Theater script binders that are quickly changed for other scripts and give a professional look to your performance.

2. Make a sign for each child in the *Hallo-wiener* group to hold up (attach to tongue depressors) as they read for clarity. The characters are Narrator 1–6, Dog 1, Dog 2, Mother, Oscar, Cat 1, and Cat 2.

Activity Directions:

1. Read the book to students. Then choose parts, distribute scripts, and allow everyone time to read over their parts.

2. *Ghost-eye Tree* is meant to be read chorally. Ask how many students have brothers/sisters that they sometimes tease or argue with. Can they think of a time when they worked together or got along especially well? Have students turn to a neighbor and tell him/her about such a time. Then, introduce the book by briefly retelling the entire story, showing students the illustrations. Divide your class into three groups—girls, boys, and several you select to read the narrator parts. Model for them how to use expression. Have a student or teacher help you model

Reader's Theater Tips

Check out www.busyteacherscafe.com/units/readers_theater.htm. This site is like having your own personal director and stage manager. Tips for finding scripts, staging the performance, and coaching your readers are included as well as a number of sources for scripts.

how to read together rather than disjointedly. Tell them this is meant to be a suspenseful story, so really put expression and feeling into it. All the boys read the boy part, all the girls read the girl part, and the narrators read their specific parts. After, lead students in a brief discussion about how the two children really cared for each other. At what point can they tell? (When the hat lands by the ghost-eye tree.)

For *Hallo-wiener,* have the teacher or yourself choose children for the 12 parts. They will perform the play for the group by reading with great zest and expression. (Model this yourself.) If there is time, switch so the audience is now reading the 12 parts and the first group listens attentively. The second performance will be even better.

3. Allow both groups to read over their scripts. Ask them to check with someone in their group to see if they know words they are unsure of. For the second play, the audience can check out books while the readers look over their scripts and get tips from you. When you switch casts, the first readers can check out while the second group reads over their parts.

4. Before the performances, tell the audience that you will be asking them what they liked about it and what could be improved. When the performances are over, ask them.

Resources:

The Ghost-eye Tree by Bill Martin Jr. and John Archambault. Henry Holt & Company, 1988, c1985.

The Hallo-wiener by Dav Pilkey. Scholastic, 1999, c1995.

Ugly Book Contest

The library has a lot of books with unattractive "costumes" or covers. Sponsor an Ugly Book Contest. See the book cover creator students can use at readwritethink.org/student_mat/student_material.asp?id=58.

Additional Lessons for October

Stretchy Library Lesson Series

Stretchy Library Lessons: Library Skills

"Genre Relay" (3–5), pp. 9–13. Relay race to sort books burns energy and enlightens brain cells. Genre Lotto directions and game board stretch the lesson.

"Meet Melvil" (3–5), pp. 38–42. Students use their bodies to remember Dewey's Divisions. Students try to generate 10 divisions into which they think written works can be sorted. Note: Change 300 to Ear: Folktales were passed down orally so we had to listen.

Stretchy Library Lessons: More Library Skills

"Earn Your Library Wings" (3–5) pp. 26–34. Five flight-related activity levels help students develop independence in locating a book by its Dewey number. It includes a pilot's log, paper airplane directions, and more.

Stretchy Library Lessons: Multicultural Activities

"Food" (K–2, 3–5), pp. 50–56. Includes patterns for *Mama Provi and the Pot of Rice,* as well as a matching game with popular foods that come from other countries.

Stretchy Library Lessons: Reading Activities

"Comprehension Climb" (2–5), pp. 63–71. Use the game board template to create a Battle Board. Includes form for students to create questions and five pages of questions for a Magic Tree House battle.

Stretchy Library Lessons: Research Skills

"Sticks and Stones" (K–2, 2–5), pp. 9–13. Use author sticks and alphabet stones to learn alphabetization to the third letter. Note: Commercially made version available from Highsmith.

"Partner Passports to PAC" (3–5), pp. 14–17. Use your library's automated catalog to answer 10 questions with a partner to earn a library passport to adventure.

"Take Note!" (3–5), pp. 29–42. Use *Mrs. Katz and Tush* to introduce note-taking. Templates and examples included for animal, famous person, and Native American notes for reports.

Stretchy Library Lessons: Seasons & Celebrations

"Hobby Month" (K–3), pp. 31–37. Chart class collections, complete a logic puzzle, match cause and effect cards from *Sylvester and the Magic Pebble,* and more.

Collaborative Bridges Series: Primary

Home Sweet Earth
"Habitats" pp. 37–44. Food chains, biome games, creature sort, and more are the subject of the activities in this unit. There's even a script for *The Lion and the Mouse* for interdependence.

It's Alive
"Living or Nonliving" pages 8–23. Students determine what's living, once living, and not living. Activities are based on growth, life cycles, matching parents with their babies, crafting a chrysalis, creating a class book, and more. Reproducibles include reporting forms for observations, sorting, simple research, and class book templates.

Collaborative Bridges Series: Intermediate
by Aileen Kirkham

Danger Zone!
"Solar System: From Cultural Curiosity to Space Travel" pp 91–111. Dramatize a Native American tale, explore Greek mythology, write Haiku, measure space weight, measure space time, and plan a space trip.

People, Places, and Things
"Mapping the World: Past, Present & Future" pp. 53–61. Use clues for map and globe skills, find international pen pals, play navigator's challenge, and create a tourism brochure.

LibrarySparks Correlation

If you are a *LibrarySparks* subscriber like me, you may overlook the great lessons in your back issues as you plan for future lessons. To help us both (part of my resolution to be more organized), each month will include references to additional lessons in *LibrarySparks* magazine. If you are not a subscriber, you still have access to the articles with an * on the *LibrarySparks* Web site: www.librarysparks.com. Every issue online and in the magazine includes a calendar with daily books, events, and suggested activities. Most are quick and easy.

October 2003 (Theme: Fall)
Meet the Author: Denise Fleming (K–2)
Storytime: Fall Draw and Tell Stories (K–2)
Creative Crafts: Monsters and Magical Creatures (K–2)
Library Lessons: Apples, Pumpkins, Research (3–5)
Curriculum Connections: Happy Halloween (K–5)
Booktalks: Spook-tacular (K–3) and (4–6)

October 2004 (Theme: Get Out the Vote)

Curriculum Connections: Elections (1–5)

Storytime: Slow Down (K–2)

Meet the Illustrator: David Small and Paired Readings: Fiction and Nonfiction with David Small (3–5)

Book Club: So You Want to Be President (3–5)

Library Lessons: A Mystery in the Library—Fribble Mouse Goes on a Library Treasure Hunt (3–5)

Contest: Match the Siblings to Their Book (3–5) *

October 2005 (Theme: Colonial America)

Storytime: Sing a Song of Scarecrows (K–2)

Celebrations: Teddy Bear Day (K–2)

Curriculum Connections: Fire Prevention Week (K–2) *

Curriculum Connections: Colonial America (3–5)

Reader's Theater: "My Name is Deborah Samson" (3–5)

Library Lessons: Key Word Searching (3–5)

Meet the Authors: Tony DiTerlizzi and Holly Black with Author Extensions for The Spiderwick Chronicles (3–5)

Keep 'em Reading: *Harry Potter and the Goblet of Fire* lessons and activities *

Research: Wild Bear Challenge (3–5) *

October 2006 (Theme: Immigrants All!)

Storytime: Super Baby! (K–2)

Storytime: Hosting a Bedtime Stories Night (K–2)

Curriculum Connections: Immigrants All! (3–5)

Reader's Theater: *Faraway Home* (3–5)

In the Spotlight: *The Boy Who Loved Words* (3–5)

Library Lessons: Owls, Bats and Spiders (Research) (1–3)

Meet the Author: James Howe (3–5)

Keep 'em Reading: Constitution Day (K–5)

Author Extensions: This Man on an Island (3–5)

Bibliography

A

Alborough, Jez. *My Friend Bear.* Candlewick Press, 2001, c1998.

B

Barner, Bob. *Dem Bones.* Chronicle Books, 1996.

Berkowitz, Jacob. *Jurassic Poop: What Dinosaurs (and Others) Left Behind.* Kids Can Press, 2006.

Bree, Loris. *Kids' Magic Secrets: Simple Magic Tricks & Why They Work.* Marlor Press, 2003.

Buttitta, Hope. *It's Not Magic, It's Science! 50 Science Tricks That Mystify, Dazzle & Astound!* Lark Books, 2005.

C

Chrisp, Peter. *Christopher Columbus: Explorer of the New World.* DK Publishing, 2006.

Codell, Esmé Raji. *How to Get Your Child to Love Reading: For Ravenous and Reluctant Readers Alike.* Algonquin Books, 2003.

Cole, Joanna. *Bony-legs.* Scholastic, 1983.

Coleman, Janet Wyman. *Famous Bears and Friends: One Hundred Years of Stories, Poems, Songs, and Heroics.* Dutton, 2002.

Collier, James Lincoln. *Christopher Columbus: To the New World.* Marshall Cavendish, 2007.

Crossingham, John, and Bobbie Kalman. *Extreme In-line Skating.* Crabtree Publishing Company, 2004.

D

DeFelice, Cynthia. *The Dancing Skeleton.* Aladdin Paperbacks, 1996, c1989.

E

Edwards, Wallace. *The Extinct Files: My Science Project.* Kids Can Press, 2006.

F

Farmer, Jacqueline. *Pumpkins.* Charlesbridge Publishing, 2004.

Faulkner, Megan. *A Day at the Pumpkin Patch.* Scholastic Canada, 2006.

Fowler, Allan. *It's a Fruit, It's a Vegetable, It's a Pumpkin.* Children's Press, 1995.

Fridell, Ron and Patricia Walsh. *Life Cycle of a Pumpkin.* Heinemann Library, 2001.

G

Grambling, Lois G. *Can I Bring My Pterodactyl to School, Ms. Johnson?* Charlesbridge Publishing, 2006.

Grambling, Lois. *Happy Valentine's Day, Miss Hildy.* Random House, 1998.

Grosgebauer, Clare. *Snickerdoodle and the Roller-Skating Horse!* Small Wonders Enterprises, 2005.

H

Hall, Kirsten. *I See a Bug.* Scholastic, 1996.

Hall, Zoe. *It's Pumpkin Time!* Blue Sky Press, 1999, c1994.

Harper, Charise Mericle. *Imaginative Inventions: The Who, What, Where, When, and Why of Roller Skates, Potato Chips, Marbles, and Pie and More!* Little, Brown and Company, 2001.

Herman, R. A. *The Littlest Pumpkin.* Scholastic, 2001.

Higgins, Nadia. *Columbus and the Age of Explorers.* Rourke Press, 2007.

Ho, Oliver. *Young Magician: Magic Tricks.* Sterling Publishing, 2003.

Hort, Lenny. *Did Dinosaurs Eat Pizza? Mysteries Science Hasn't Solved.* Henry Holt & Company, 2006.

Hutchings, Amy and Richard. *Picking Apples & Pumpkins.* Scholastic, 1994.

K

Kimmel, Eric A. *Anansi and the Magic Stick.* Holiday House, 2001.

King, Elizabeth. *The Pumpkin Patch.* Puffin, 1996, c1990.

Klingel, Cynthia, and Robert Noyed. *Card Tricks.* Compass Point Books, 2002.

Kottke, Jan. *From Seed to Pumpkin.* Children's Press, 2000.

Kroll, Steven. *The Biggest Pumpkin Ever.* Scholastic, 1984.

L

Levenson, George. *Pumpkin Circle: The Story of a Garden.* Tricycle Press, 2002, c1999.

M

Martin, Jr., Bill, and John Archambault. *The Ghost-eye Tree.* Henry Holt & Company, 1988, c1985.

McNamara, Margaret. *The Pumpkin Patch.* Aladdin Paperbacks, 2003.

N

Nagel, Karen Berman. *Two Crazy Pigs.* Scholastic, 1992.

Nikola-Lisa, W. *Shake Dem Halloween Bones.* Houghton Mifflin, 1997.

Noonan, Julia. *My Pumpkin.* Children's Press, 2005.

P

Pfeffer, Wendy. *From Seed to Pumpkin.* HarperCollins, 2004.

Pilkey, Dav. *The Hallo-wiener.* Scholastic, 1999, c1995.

Polacco, Patricia. *Mrs. Katz and Tush.* Dell Dragonfly Books, 1994, c1992.

Prats, Joan de Deu. *Sebastian's Roller Skates.* Kane/Miller Book Publishers, 2005.

R

Richardson, Adele. *Bears: Paws, Claws, and Jaws.* Bridgestone Books, 2001.

Robbins, Ken. *Pumpkins.* Roaring Brook Press, 2006.

Rosa-Casanova, Sylvia. *Mama Provi and the Pot of Rice.* Atheneum, 1997.

S

Sadler, Marilyn. *P. J. Funnybunny's Bag of Tricks.* Random House, 2004.

Sheldon, David. *Barnum Brown, Dinosaur Hunter.* Walker & Co., 2006.

Standiford, Natalie. *The Stone Giant: A Hoax that Fooled America.* Golden Books, 2001.

Steig, William. *Sylvester and the Magic Pebble.* Simon & Schuster, 2005, c1969.

T

Titherington, Jeanne. *Pumpkin, Pumpkin.* Greenwillow Books, 1986.

V

Van Rynback, Iris. *Five Little Pumpkins.* Mills Press, 2003, c1995.

W

Wallace, Nancy Elizabeth. *Pumpkin Day!* Marshall Cavendish, 2002.

Watts, Barrie. *Pumpkin.* Smart Apple Media, 2003.

Woods, Bob. *In-line Skating.* Gareth Stevens, 2004.

Y

Yolen, Jane. *Encounter.* Harcourt Brace, 1992.

Z

Zion, Gene. *Harry the Dirty Dog.* HarperCollins, 2002, c1956.